Koffi

The darker the secret
The sweeter the revenge!

This is a work of fiction. Names, characters, places events and incidents are used for the Author's imagination and used fictionally.

Library of Congress Control Number: 2010924838
ISBN 10: 0-9826652-7-X
ISBN 13: 978-0-9826652-7-5
Cover Designed: DESIGNS BY NEESHA
Editor: Abstract Mind Publishing

Printed in the United States of America

Copyright©2015 Sheridan Brown Press

KOFFI

PROLOGUE...

$\mathcal{R}$ochelle was a feisty and vibrant seventeen year old that was not well liked by some of the girls within the neighborhood. She was not so well liked because people saw her fair skin and her beauty, and their immediate perception was that she was too much. What some didn't know was that opposite was true. Rochelle was ashamed of her roots due to the fact that her parents were a mixed couple. That was something that was frowned upon in the seventies. Rochelle stood five feet five inches tall; her shoulder length jet-black hair was inherited directly from her dad's African American and Indian roots. Her lean frame derived from her mother, who wanted to be a model, that dream never came to fruition. Rochelle's mom was white and as a result Rochelle had very fair skin.

The girls in the neighborhood hated her, because they wanted to be like her and the guys all fawned over her because they wanted her. On her way home from the store, she was approached by Mitchell, the town's rich kid. He thought that every girl wanted him and found him irresistible, but as far as Rochelle was concerned nothing was further from the truth. She did not care about him or his so-called friends. Other girls would get all goofy and crazy over him, but she did not. She could have cared less. He was a handsome dude, tall, dark as night and probably every girls dream. Rochelle had heard the rumors of him and his bad boy reputation. Rochelle made it her mission to stay far away from him and the likes of him.

One sunny afternoon, when school was over Mitchell laid eyes on Rochelle and noticed she was walking alone; he looked to his left and to his right making sure the coast was clear as he approached her. With his smooth walk like his father, he approached Rochelle from the back and grabbed her around her waist. A shocked Rochelle quickly pushed his hand away and turned to see who it was that was invading her space. When she caught sight of Mitchell and noticed that he was alone, her senses heightened and kicked into overdrive. Something in her told her that he was up to no good and to be on alert. He eased his hand around her shoulder and continued to try to walk with her; she stopped cold in her tracks and questioned what he was doing. He tried his best to make her think everything was all good, when in actuality he had dirt on the brain. He then started to look up and down the street and decided that now was as good a time as any to pull this caper off. On the corner was an empty abandoned building that was perfect for what he had planned. Mitchell grabbed Rochelle by her ponytail inside the building and pulled her into a funk filled room. The stench from the building was that of Jack Daniels and old cigarettes from the local besotted homeless in which they respectfully referred to as home. Mitchell looked at her with the lust of a pervert before he threatened her. He told her to shut up and let him have his way, if she didn't he would tell everyone that she tried to come on to him. Rochelle knew he meant every word.

Forced on the dirty floor, the sweat from Mitchell's forehead began to drip down onto Rochelle's hard nipples that were protruding through her thin white shirt; he then forced her onto her stomach which left her perfect rounded bottom adjacent to his erect manhood. He began to whisper obscenities in her ear. He called her all kinds of filthy sluts and mutt bitches. Rochelle, who was in shock about what was happening to her, did not shed a tear. Apparently Mitchell thought she wanted it because he was able to continue his assault on her body. He was roughly running his hands up and down her body as he reached under her skirt and tore her panties away in a swift and brief motion. Rochelle still did not retreat; she let him continue to have his way with her. It was not until he finished, that she had finally grasped reality and what was going on around her. When he did finish he made sure that he left his whole load in her. He smiled a wicked smile as he got up and buckled his belt. He looked down at her with a sick smirk on his face and just before turning to leave he told her if she breathes a word of this to anyone, he would make her life a living hell. Little did he know, that was already done.

The once beautiful and vibrant Rochelle became a shell of a young lady. She noticed subtle changes in her body, attitude and appetite weeks and even months after the rape. One week she took her allowance and went to the five and dime store she purchased a pregnancy test. She knew she could not go home and take the test without arousing her grandmother's' suspicions, so she made her way to the back of the store and used the bathroom there. What she saw 5 minutes later, made her breath catch in her throat. Her mind went into overdrive, trying to figure out how she was going to tell her grandmother. She knew that if she told her then she should be admitting that Mitchell raped her and she was not ready to face that demon. She quietly wept as she tossed the test, the box and all its contents in the trash and made her way out of the bathroom.

Just shy of turning eighteen she knew she would have to live with this experience for the rest of her life and her dreams of attending college are all out the window. This is not at all what she pictured her first time to be like. Although she was feisty and full of life, she walked the walk and talked the talk. She was a virgin, something her friends could not say. That was the one thing she was proud of, and now that is all gone. To add insult to injury she had to hide this unwanted pregnancy from all of her friends and most importantly her grandmother. Besides, what would her grandmother think of her being barely an adult, still in school, and pregnant?

She knew that her grandmother would soon look at her the way she looked at her mom. She already knew her mom was a whore and that she was left with her grandmother so she can whore around. Rochelle hated her mother because of this. She hated her dad, because although he took care of her, he never spent any time with her. He would drop by month after month and bring her grandmother checks, food and clothes for Rochelle, but he never spent more than five minutes in her presence. She knew that her dad was married and her mom tricked him. Her mom apparently thought her being pregnant would make him leave his wife. That was far from the truth, he did however make sure she was taken care of.

As she was making her way out the five and dime she ran into the person

she knew she did not want to see,
Mitchell. He was with is homeboys and
she looked him in the eyes ready to say
sorry when her words choked her and
she started to gag and thew up right near
his fresh gators. His boys all looked on
with amused looks on their faces. He just
looked at her pushed her out the way
and told her watch where she was going.
She scurried away quickly, but not
before he could say something to her
that reminded her that he had hurt her
once and he would not hesitate to do it
again.

Rochelle found it relatively easy
to hide her pregnancy from her

grandmother and friends. She did not show much and as time went by she started filling out in different places and not the stomach. She was in the shower one day and her grandmother walked in the bathroom on her. Her secret was out. Her grandmother had a fit and called her every name in the book. This made Rochelle more and more depressed. She had decided that she would not stick around and be a burden to her grandmother. After she showered, she dressed and took to the street. She slept in building after building, eating what she could when she could.

Instead of going back home to tell her grandmother what really happened, she decided to brave the streets. She soon realized the streets were no place for a pregnant girl. She wondered into an old abandoned building just off Eighth and Chestnut. She was cold, tired and eventually she fell asleep on the cold floor. A few hours had past, and Rochelle began to feel sharp pains ripping through her body. The first pain stirred her, but that second one made her sit straight up. Rochelle began to yelp in pain as she felt a warm liquid gush from between her legs.

Since no one ever told her about labor, she assumed the worse. She began trying to get up from the floor and another pain stabbed her pulling her back down to the floor. She finally mustered up enough energy and made her way to the door. She peeked out the door and looked around the corners to see if there was anyone standing around, anyone that would help her. She saw no one and took a step outside and from the first step and another pain went coursing through her body.

Rochelle attempted the five block walk to the nearest hospital, while she was walking the pains started coming one after the next. A time or two she had the overwhelming desire to move her bowels, but unbeknownst to her, she was in the final stages of labor. By the time she was two blocks from the hospital, a weak and frail Rochelle fell face down to the ground in tears and defeat. She was too weak to carry on and much too weak to cry out for help. A passerby in a light blue Chevy saw her kneeling down and jumped from his car, running to her aid. He pulled up at the hospital's emergency room in time to deliver a feeble and fatigued Rochelle to the nurse's station.

Rochelle had given birth to a six pound, five ounce baby girl. The baby girl was beautiful and was the darkest baby Rochelle had ever seen. She looked at her daughter and turned away, she was a reminder that she was not conceived out of love and it was at that moment that Rochelle decided she did not want to have anything else to do with her. She did name the baby and that was the end of her connection with her daughter. She named the baby Koffi, that is just what she saw when she looked at her, so that name was suitable.

For days the nurses tried to get Rochelle to at least breastfeed, with the hopes that she would bond with Koffi and change her mind about not wanting her. They were sadly mistaken; she turned away each time they tried to bring her into the room. In the following days Rochelle started to feel better and stronger, she got up and left the hospital against doctors' orders.

Koffi was placed with the state and was in state care until she made six months of age. Koffi became the temporary foster child of Stanley and Rebecca Hinson. When Koffi turned four she was adopted out of the system completely by the Hinson's. The Hinson's however did allow her to keep her last name of Simpson.

As Koffi got older, her curiosity about her mom grew. She was itching to know where she came from. The Hinson's did not hide the fact that she was adopted and answered all her curious questions to the best of their abilities. While Stanley was dead set against her knowing, Rebecca always thought she had the right to know where she came from.

Koffi loved her foster mother Rebecca, but she started to grow an innate hatred toward Stanley. It started when she was about twelve years old. Her body had just started filling out and she was feeling so awkward about it. Of all the girls in class she had to have the longest hair, biggest ass, biggest titties and the flattest stomach. Once while she was bathing Stanley stumbled into the bathroom on her. In her twelve year old mind it was an accident but when she had time to really think on it she knew it was not, because he knew what time she took her bath every night unless it was a weekend. This just so happened to be a time when Rebecca was not home.

By the time Koffi was fifteen, a rage had taken over her soul and as a result every relationship she entered in was toxic. Koffi was a very intelligent young lady, she never used drugs, never picked up a drink and she loved school with a passion. School proved to be her escape from the hell she was living in at the Hinson's. Koffi did in fact have one weakness, and that was older, working married men. Men that could provide her with the lavish things she knew boys her age could not provide her with. So she just wondered, why bother with them. Stanley set the standard because he started paying for it. First it went from touching, to feeling, to cuddling, to fondling to full out tantric sex. He paid Koffi handsomely to do the things Rebecca would not even think of doing. Stanley knew good and damn well what he was doing was wrong. So from that point on, any older married man willing to pay, was not off limits to Koffi.

Koffi had become pregnant at the age of sixteen, and lost the baby. It wasn't two years later that she was indeed pregnant again. Rebecca stuck by her side and did all she could to make Koffi comfortable in her pregnancy. That was until she delivered and the awful truth was revealed. The truth that stuck out was Stanley was the father of Koffi's son, Lance.

This hurt Rebecca to her core. She began to wonder back to when and how it could have happened. She remembered the times when Stanley would send her on errands that he would usually run himself. Times when he insisted that he was not emerging from Koffi's room on the countless nights she saw him coming from that direction. So many times she witnessed things, and Rebecca missed all the signs. Of the truth.

On her eighteenth birthday, Koffi received the gift of a lifetime. Rebecca had found out about Rochelle's where-a-bouts, that was news that left Koffi feeling some kind of way. She knew that all the love Rebecca had for her went out the window when Lance was born. Koffi gathered all the information that Rebecca shared and she started on the hunt for Rochelle. Little did she know she did not have far to look. Rochelle had been right under her nose all along. In Koffi's mind, she tried to convince herself that she was not holding any anger toward her mother, but the decisions that Koffi made in life told a very different story.

Koffi still had a hunger inside her, an insatiable desire to find out all she could about her family. If she had to turn over sticks and stones to do it, then so be it. Koffi went on this mission leaving the Hinson's house and never looking back.

KOFFI

CHAPTER I...

Shit, I'm late! I had only twenty minutes to get across town to the soup kitchen to get my groceries before heading off to work, Koffi hit the snooze button at least twice this morning.

"Lance baby, it's time to get up," she yelled across her room.

She hated to get her son up this early, but she had no choice in the matter. Little Lance wiped the sleep from his eyes got out of his little Spiderman bed, and headed to the corner to wash up.

"I don't want to Mommy, I'm tired."

"I know baby, but you know Mommy has to do this or we won't eat when we get home later, Please, just be patient with Mommy, okay?"

"Okay Mommy, I will."

Koffi hated this part of her day. She had to get up extra early to get her groceries and then come right back to her room just to be to work on time. This was her daily routine. Koffi never went out, never saw friends, and she had no steady man in her life. Her son, Lance, did have many "uncles". She hated the things she had to do just to make ends meet or just to feed Lance and herself, but she did it anyway.

It was the middle of January and thirty-six degrees outside, but felt more like ten degrees. Koffi made sure Lance was bundled up, put on her wool trench coat, and started to make her way to the soup kitchen. Harmony Hands Kitchen was about four blocks away from where she and Lance stayed. Koffi always made sure she was at least the tenth person in line, because if she were any later, she would not be able to feed her son. Koffi started down the stairs as quietly as possible, in an attempt not to awaken Mrs. Blackstone, who was the property owner. She did not pay her room fee yet and she knew it would be just a matter of time before Mrs. Blackstone started in on her for money.

"Where do you think you're going young lady?" Mrs. Blackstone, the owner of where Koffi stayed never missed a beat when it came to Koffi.

"Morning Mrs. Blackstone; I was actually just coming to talk to you," was all the Koffi could muster up as she rolled her eyes up toward the ceiling, in an attempt to hide both her embarrassment and the shame that came with not being able to pay rent on time.

"I hope about my money. You know Koffi, you think I don't know what you're up to; However, I do. I know everything that goes on around here. So where's my money?"

"I promise I'm going to have your money later this evening. I just need to work a few hours and I will be able to pay you. Please just give me until tonight?" Koffi pleaded.

Mrs. Blackstone spit her tobacco in her cup and gave Koffi an evil glare. "You lucky I'm sweet on this cute little boy of yours. I want my money Koffi, Tonight!" Mrs. Blackstone went back into her apartment without a care in the world.

Koffi just looked down at her son and started to make her way out into the cold toward the Soup Kitchen. She knew she had better come up with the money or she would find herself out on the street.

"Well hello again! What do you need today?" He said, with a smile of an angel.

"What do you have today?" Koffi said to Mr. Giselle, half owner of Harmony Hands took her plastic bags and started to put groceries inside them. Koffi could feel his wife's eyes glaring as if she wanted to kill her. But then again, she got that from any woman whose man paid her any attention sometimes a simple hello would end up with all hell breaking loose and Koffi fighting somebody because their man is disrespectful.

"Oh just give her the damn groceries, Greg! Don't you see that her son is hungry, Hurry up!" Mrs. Giselle never liked the extra attention her husband always gave Koffi. Her insecurities were very clear and it showed every time Koffi shopped there. If she only knew that Koffi did not want her husband, but Koffi knew from his conversations and actions that he lusted over her.

"Thank you Mr. Giselle; I really do appreciate your kindness and yours as well Mrs. Giselle. I'm so glad that you are open this early, otherwise I would be late for work." Koffi tried to appease her whenever she felt the tension, but inside, she just wanted to beat the living shit out of her insecure ass. Koffi was no fool either; she knew that if she really did what she wanted to do she would be out of luck. Then how would she feed Lance? So instead she just chilled and let her have her way. But not without laying it on extra thick with Mr. Giselle before parting from the couple's company.

Andrea and Greg Giselle come from what is called old money, but between the two, you would never know who had it. Koffi heard about them from Mrs. Blackstone who knew everyone's business around town. However, it was very clear to Koffi that Andrea wore the pants in this marriage. Andrea snatched the bag out of Greg's hands and threw it towards Koffi. "Well I guess you better get on your way then. Take your little brat with you, before you are late for your beloved job," she said with a sly smirk on her face.

"Excuse me, did you just call my son a brat?" Koffi balled up her fist as no one ever disrespects her son, and no within her presence.

She pushed Lance behind her and she slowly yet steadily moved towards Andrea. She felt a tug on the back of her coat, just before she reached her target. She looked down and Lance who looked up at her with pleading eyes just then she was brought back to reality. She stared at Andrea with a sinister smirk thinking 'my son just saved your ass.' Andrea looked at her with bulging eyes as she scampered behind her husband who was now trying to figure out what happened in such a short time frame. Greg already knew that one of these days Andrea's sarcastic mouth was going to overload her ass and it seems like today was just that day. Greg was happy as shit to see someone stand up to Andrea, he knew from experience that she was all bark and no bite. So he reveled in the fact that someone was about to dig in her ass.

"Be glad I didn't call him something else! You come in here looking like a whore and expect a handout. There are people here that really need it, but from the looks of you, I don't think you do. You are lucky my husband feels sorry for you, otherwise I would give you the same scraps I give to my dog. Now move it along so we can serve people that really need it." Andrea's words stung.

Greg just dropped his head in shame, the fact that Andrea thought it was her job to judge people based on their circumstances always pissed him off to no end. He really wanted Koffi to wipe the floor with his wife but then he thought what kind of husband would sit back and let another woman beat his wife. He quickly turned to her and told her to shut up that she was making a scene. Andrea tried to avoid Koffi's icy glare as she peered around her husband to look out into the crowd at the other patrons. Just as Greg was talking to Andrea Koffi had decided she has had enough, she looked over at The Giselle's and then down at Lance. In that moment she let all of her senses go out the window. She would figure out how to feed Lance later but today she had an itch that needed to be scratched.

She looked down at Lance, "Lance, baby, take this bag and wait outside for Mommy, do not move until I come outside to get you, I will be right out, ok baby?"

"Yes Mommy" Lance looking at her with big brown wide hopeful eyes.

As soon as Koffi saw that her son was completely out the front door, she leaped over the counter and commenced to whoop Andrea's ass like she was a man! She did not even see it coming. Each time she swung, Koffi's right hand met her face. Before either Greg or Andrea could register what was going on, Koffi had already had Andrea by her long hair and was delivering nothing but haymakers to her face. Greg noticed that Koffi was getting the best of Andrea and he wanted to break it up, he noticed the onlookers and he hesitated for a second before yelling for them to stop the madness. Greg kept screaming for them to stop, but Koffi was not giving in. He looked around the shop and spotted a strong looking gentleman and motioned for him to come and help break the ladies up. As the crowd was growing close around the fight, the man moved with swiftness to help Greg try to pry the two ladies apart. Andrea finally had it coming to her. Koffi had years of frustration and pain all built up in her and she was finally releasing it on Andrea.

"Ladies, ladies stop this!" Greg screamed as he was trying to pull them apart.

Greg tried to pull Koffi off his wife, but she had a strong grip on Andrea's long hair. The man that Greg called over was able to finally get Andrea away from Koffi's grasp. When Andrea was freed, she retreated to the back of the store like the coward she was.

"Go straight to hell you Jezebel if I ever catch you in here again, I will have you arrested, get out, get the hell out!" Andrea enraged, wiped the blood from her bottom lip, and pushed through the rest of the patrons in the store to get out of their eyesight.

"I got your Jezebel bitch, let me go," Koffi was ready to charge at her again, but Greg was holding on to her, so that she could not get to his wife. Greg grabbed Koffi's arm and escorted Koffi to the front entrance where Lance was waiting for her.

"I'm sorry about my wife; she is jealous of any woman around me. Where did you learn to fight like that?" he asked, amused with what went down a few minutes ago.

"I'm not sure which part you found funny, the part about me beating her ass or the part that I actually beat her ass?" Koffi said with a smirk on her face. "No one and I mean no one disrespects my son. I'm sorry I beat her up like that, but every time I come in here she's always messing with me!"

Greg grabbed Koffi's hand "I'm sorry for her attitude. She is like that with any woman that I pay attention to. Maybe I could still help you if you let me."

His eyes were deadlocked on Koffi's low cut, wool V-neck sweater that exposed her perky 36D cup breasts. She could tell he wanted more than to just help her. He made it known with little subtle gestures and the tones in which he spoke to her. Koffi had always been curious about Greg's interest in her, but now she was sure. She wanted to tell him, that he had nothing to apologize for, Andrea is a grown woman and that she is responsible for her own actions. Desperate times called for desperate measures.

"Listen, I don't want any trouble with your wife. I promise you next time you will not be able to pull me off her, but you said you wanted to help me out, all I want to know is how can you help me?" Koffi grabbed little Lance's hand so they could begin the cold walk back to their room.

Greg walked closer to her and they were face to face, and with that gesture their lips almost touched. He stood just a few inches taller than Koffi and smelled so damn good. Koffi was not attracted to him, but he was making it hard for her not to be. It did not matter that it was almost freezing outside because her body was overheating internally. She was feeling like a fire was blazing right underneath her. The closer he came to her, the wetter and hotter she got. *What's wrong with you Koffi; this man is married!* She

silently cursed herself. *You can't do this,
you just can't!* Her body was giving her
all kinds of reasons to do what she
wanted with this man, even if it was
wrong. But her mind was telling her
something totally different. She looked
down at Lance who was shifting his
weight from one foot to the next in an
effort to stay warm, but most of all
remain patient while his soon to be
"Uncle" finished whispering sweet
nothings to his mom. She told him to
take the bags and start walking toward
the room that the two of them shared.
Lance did as he was told.

"Well since it is a little cold out and you are headed to drop your son off before you head off to work yourself, can I stop by your room later, and I can show you what I mean by wanting to help you out. I am a man of action and not talk." Greg grabbed Koffi's hand and slowly moved his thumb up and down softly inside the palm of her hand.

His touch felt so good that Koffi imagined what it would feel like if he were inside of her. He had broad shoulders and always dressed in suits or an argyle sweater. He always wore expensive cologne and never the same one. When he took off his glasses, he resembled a lighter version of Morris Chestnut. Koffi never saw herself with him because he seemed very needy. Koffi ached for a strong confident man. She needed a man that will take control and take care of his woman. She took Greg's hand, pushed up the sleeve of his sweater and wrote her address on his forearm. She did it this way so that Andrea would not see it once he went inside. Greg dipped his hands in his pocket right after that and came up with a wad of bills. He peeled off a few hundreds and some fifties and handed them to her and told her this should hold her for a while and if she was as good as he anticipated there will be more where that had come from. He then slowly started walking backward toward the center, when he heard the annoying voice of Andrea.

"Greg, Greg, are you still out here with her, I need your help in here now!" Andrea had come running outside after realizing Greg was still outside with Koffi. She hated him helping any woman, especially Koffi. Greg went back inside to help her, but he definitely made Koffi know that he will be putting that address to good use later that night.

Koffi had put some pep in her step to catch up with Lance, who was waiting for her at the corner. Lance questioned her with his eyes before asking, "Momma can we go home now, I'm cold, and I still have to get my bag for school and you have to get your work stuff." He was rubbing his little cold hands together trying to keep them warm.

"Yes baby, let's go." As Koffi turned to walk away, she glanced back at Greg with a smile on her face as she thought about what excuse he would give his wife. Regardless of the excuse that would be given, Koffi would make sure Greg would never regret it.

KOFFI

CHAPTER II...

The walk home was brutal. Koffi's little tan wool woven trench coat was nothing compared to the icy cold wind. Although it was 36 degrees out, with the wind chill factor, it felt more like 10. The way the wind gusts began to pick up you would think she was wrapped in plastic and not a wool coat. She had no to time to think of that now, she knew Lance was cold, and she felt like a piece of shit taking him with her, but she could not allow him to stay by himself in the room. Last time she did that, Mrs. Blackstone threatened to call

Child Services on her. She grasped the jacket tightly around her neck as she and Lance trekked back to the room. She thought about the money that Greg had given her; she did not want to seem too pressed so she just decided she will wait until she was in the warmth of her room to count it. She silently hoped that it was enough to get Mrs. Blackstone off of her back for at least a week or two. Koffi had known by the tone that Mrs. Blackstone had taken with her earlier that she was very serious about throwing her and her baby out in the cold, no matter how cute Lance was. Koffi also knew that her son being cute did not pay the bills. She was well aware of this first hand. She vowed that Lance would be taken care of by any means necessary. As Koffi was making her way up the stairs to the safety of her room she started to think about how she needed to get money and fast so that she and Lance could get escape the hell that was slowly engulfing their lives.

She had a neighbor by the name of Peter, and word around town was that Peter was a pervert but he did not like girls or the women in the building, he was smitten with little boys. She saw Peter look at Lance one time too many with that, 'I cannot wait to be alone with him look.' Peter even thought a time or two that Koffi was a fool; he offered to keep Lance while one of Lance's "Uncles" was visiting. Koffi Knew by the eagerness in his voice that he was up to no good. She remembered that one time she did go on a quick run to the corner store and she left Lance in her room because he was asleep, she returned to see her door had been tampered with and she knew it was no one but Peter because only Mrs. Blackstone and Peter knew he was in the room. Ever since then she never left him alone again.

Upon returning home, Koffi tried to tip toe past Mrs. Blackstone's apartment, but it did not work. The strong wind had slammed the front door so hard it woke up Mrs. Blackstone along with several other tenants. "I need my money, you are not special. You have to pay your room rent like everyone else,"

A frustrated Koffi uttered out a long frustrated sigh before responding, "Look I told you woman I would have your money tonight, it's not even mid-morning yet and you already tripping. I swore I would have it and I will. Just let me get Lance off to school and then to work and I promise as soon as I am off tonight I will pay what I owe and hopefully more." Koffi was thinking back to the money Greg had given her that she had yet to count.

Mrs. Blackstone took a long drag from her cigarette, resting her tongue on her top lip, before she looked Koffi square in the eye and pointed at her with the hand that was holding the cigarette; she was exhaling smoke as she spoke to her in a tone that resembled a threat. Koffi knew full well that she could not afford to mess this up and went to her room to get ready for the day ahead.

It was already seven-thirty, and Lance was scrambling trying to get his homework inside his book bag while his mom, Koffi sat on the bed and pulled

out the money that Greg had given her.
She started counting and when she made
it to ten one hundred dollar bills and the
four fifty dollar bills, a smile of gratitude
emerged upon her face. Not only did she
have enough to pay Mrs. Blackstone and
keep her off her back for a while but she
could splurge on Lance, something she
rarely had a chance to do. She went to
the corner of the mattress and told Lance
to turn his back, she fished out an old
crown royal bag from a hole she had cut
into her mattress, and she took the four
fifties and put them inside. With the two
hundred dollars she just put away, that
brought her total life savings to two

hundred and twenty-five dollars. She folded that bag up so small and put it right back in its hiding spot.

Koffi got off the bed and changed into her work uniform. She hated wearing this uniform, but her boss demanded it. The place where she worked was called Massey's Tavern and Koffi was the best damned waitress they had ever seen. They had to wear maid-like uniforms and because of her voluptuous shape, her tips would always be the highest of all the other girls there. The hatred for Koffi whenever she came to work was very apparent with all the other girls. Koffi knew she had to do what she had to do to make claim on what was rightfully hers.

She then grabbed Lance and headed out the door for work. Her mind on Greg and what he had expected for the money he gave her. She quickly dismissed that thought when she remembered all the drama from this morning. As she was descending the stairs, she saw some of the tenants milling around down stairs in the lobby. Some she knew was expecting a show from Mrs. Blackstone. Mrs. Blackstone loved to put on a show for her tenants but she was reserved with Koffi and Lance.

Green Gardens was a twenty room boarding house with five rooms to each floor. Every room had one full-sized bed, one closet with no door, a sink, one bathroom with a tub, and one window. The hallways were dusty and the floorboards creaked because they were old. The building was old and was originally built during the civil war times during 1862. Originally the building housed felons, prostitutes, drug addicts, and mentally ill residents. But over time this became known as a boarding house for anyone looking to have a place to stay or just passing through town. In some cases a felon or two would end up there, but other than that all that remained were the long-standing tenants she had. Because this place was on subsidy from the state, there had to be curfew laws set. Curfew was two-o'clock in the morning and if you broke it, or came in under the influence, Mrs. Blackstone called the cops and had you escorted off the property by the cops.

Every room had its own number and the mail was delivered to Mrs. Blackstone personally. Mrs. Blackstone and her daughter Vernell, hand delivered the mail to the tenants or would slide it under the door if they were not home when the mail was delivered. Room payments were due by the fifteenth of every month and they could not go more than five days late or the room would be bolted shut until it was paid. Mrs. Blackstone took a special interest in Koffi and her son. For reasons unknown, even though Koffi was always late, her room never was bolted.

"Mrs. Blackstone, May I have a word with you in private, please. I just want to run something by you real quick before I get my baby off to school." Koffi began to dig into her pockets and pull off two of the ten one hundred dollar bills that Greg had given her.

Koffi knew this was enough to hold her over for this month and next. She was not worried about how she would cover month after, all she knew is she and Lance were ok for these two. She would cross month after bridge when she came to it.

"Time is money, Koffi! You know if I do it for you then I have to do it for someone else. You lucky I like that sweet little boy of yours otherwise both of you would be on the street, Well did you get your groceries?" She was going on and on and she was walking to a nearby corner to talk to Koffi, out of earshot of the other people that had gathered in the foyer of the building.

She tried to act like she had in in for Koffi, when in all actuality she did not. She just could not let it show around other tenants, because they would be expecting the same type of treatment. She really did harbor a deep liking for Koffi and her son. That is one reason why she never made good on any of the threats she made to Koffi, about putting her out. The other reason is because Koffi's life was hard enough without her adding to it. Mrs. Blackstone and Koffi had history and she knew that

Koffi was facing hard times now, before then Koffi paid on time each month.

"Yes ma'am, we did, thank you for asking."

Koffi began to reach inside her pockets when she noticed Peter out the corner or her eye moving toward Lance. She backtracked and snatched Lance over to the corner with her and Mrs. Blackstone, all while giving Peter that, 'I wish a nigga would look.' She knew that if she took any longer she and Lance would both be late, she hurriedly gave Mrs. Blackstone the two hundred dollars, told her thanks and that they would talk when she returned from work. Mrs. Blackstone stood stoic and shocked, not only had Koffi paid the rent but she paid an advance on next months as well. Koffi was saying her thank yous as she was dragging Lance out the door with her.

"Thanks for giving me more time Mrs. Blackstone, I really appreciate it."

"Since you are running late for work, leave Lance here and I will have Vernell drop him off at school. She has to go by the pharmacy for me anyway and his school is right on the way. Don't worry about getting him home either, I will pick him up because I know tonight is your late night and don't worry he will stay with me until you get home to tuck him in." she kneeled down to an already smiling Lance and asked, "How does that sound?"

Lance looked up at Mrs. Blackstone all wide-eyed and innocent smiling from ear to ear. He knew he was in for a treat. On the nights when Koffi worked late he would stay with her and she would let him do what he wanted and she would feed him all the snacks and junk he could handle. If Koffi knew she would have a stroke, but Lance and Mrs. Blackstone figured what she did not know wouldn't hurt her. Koffi prided herself on being a good mother and making sure Lance was clean and well fed. That was all she could muster, considering she could not afford all the toys and things little boys like Lance wanted.

After Koffi left Lance with Mrs. Blackstone's, she headed to the bus stop. Koffi was deep in thought while walking; she did not even notice the late model Lincoln Town Car following her. She looked up just in time to see the driver smile that dashing smile that he smiled earlier. Greg had come by the house to get her when he saw her rushing from the house in a hurry to get to the bus stop. He just decided instead of making himself known that he would just follow her in hopes that she would miss the bus so that he can take her to her final destination.

The City of Beaufort right on the outskirts of South Carolina, with a population of about 12,000 and only about 5,000 who were African Americans, is where Mrs. Blackstone's boarding house resided. If you were fortunate enough to grow up here, you either worked for someone, worked at a market or owned your own market. The winter months here were moderate; and summers ranged from pleasant to hot and filled with drama. Everyone knew everyone but, more importantly, everyone knew everybody's business. The rich ran all the shops in town, yet they did not mind mingling with the average on occasion, just as long as you did not mess with them or their business. Homes here were built way back during the civil war and quite a few were still in good condition. This is where Rochelle's life thrived and Koffi became a secret.

KOFFI

CHAPTER III...

"Greg, why are you always helping that girl, she is nothing but trouble and a whore! I'm telling you, Greg, you're going to make me kill somebody over you," Andrea said, as she was counting the money from the register.

"Oh will you relax; you know that you are the only woman for me. Besides, that young woman just needs guidance and a little help. You know she came to this town alone and with a little boy. Everyone needs help at some point Andrea."

"Well why does it have to be my husband, Can you answer me that Greg?" Andrea said with a serious and disappointing look. She knew Greg hated that she was so insecure; it was just sometimes she could not hide it, and this was one of those times. Andrea gave Greg a sheepish look, that was her 'I need money look'. Greg knew that look all too well he just dug in his pocket to retrieve his wallet, he gave her a handful of bills.

"Sounds like you're jealous and you have no reason to be. I love you and only you, Okay," Greg responded.

Andrea knew her husband meant every word he said but she still was not convinced. Something told her deep within her soul that Koffi was a special kind of trouble. Koffi was the kind of trouble that she found out first hand that she wanted no parts of. She knew her kind and she was not going to let Koffi get her claws into her husband. Andrea had fought long and hard to get and keep Greg, and she would be damned if Koffi or any other whore for that matter took her place, even if it was just temporary.

"Yes baby, I know you love me and you know that I love you too, but I had better not see her again or there is going to be some serious consequences to pay. Greg, I hope you are listening to me."

Greg and Andrea worked all day down at the soup kitchen until closing. They had let all their workers go home except one and it was just the two of them. Since it was just the two of them, Andrea decided to give Greg a little surprise to make sure he understood where she was coming from. She yelled over her shoulder to let out the last worker and to meet her in the back after he had done so.

"Goodnight Andrea and Greg, See you in the morning." One of the last of the workers shouted from the front door as they left.

"See you in the morning, Jim," Greg replied, as he followed behind him and locked up.

Greg turned the open sign around from open to closed and then locked the door. As he pulled the shade down from the front windows, he looked up, what he saw shocked him.

Andrea stood near the counter covered in nothing but her apron. Greg had the look of pure lust in his eyes. He started moving slowly toward her and she put up a hand to halt him. She told him not to come any further. Andrea seductively walked toward Greg while peeling the apron from her body as she let her nakedness come close to Greg. Greg scooped her up and ran into the back office like the front of the store was on fire. If there was one thing Andrea was good at, it was pleasing her husband. This time her reason for pleasing him was because of her own selfishness. Whatever he wanted sexually, she provided willingly, no matter what. Sometimes she had to take control, but he loved every minute of her aggression.

Greg raised an eyebrow as he looked down at his wife with pure lust, not love but lust. He knew her reasons for wanting to have her way with him and he was willing to go the distance. But tonight he had something else on the agenda. Greg thought back to his college days on how he would get 'one' out of the way before the main event that made him 'go' longer. As much as he hated it, he was about to use Andrea for his 'one'. Koffi was worth him going longer for.

Greg slowly laid her on the desk that she had prepared for them, he turned her over and arched her derriere up to face him, just as he was about to dig deep, Andrea changed the game. She swiftly turned around and got on her knees. She undid his zipper with her teeth and snatched at his slacks until she heard the button pop and roll into the corner of the room. She took his tool out and began to hungrily swallow him. Andrea knew she was not a deep throater but she was willing to do anything to keep him from spilling all is jizz on Koffi. She was devouring his manhood to the point that she did not notice that moans of pleasure was becoming groans of aggravation. She was so busy obsessing on Koffi that she did not notice she was scathing Greg's manhood.

Greg jumped back and looked at Andrea like she was crazy, he decided that he'll make this a session that she will never forget. He snatched her up by her shoulder, bent her over the desk so that she was standing on the balls of her feet, he placed his hands on both of her supple ass cheeks before aiming for his target. He fired off three good long strokes; strokes that he knew drove Andrea crazy. After the long strokes, he short stroked her, on that last thrust, Greg's dick slipped; when it did he accidently hit her anal cavity. That sparked a light in him like never before.

He was ramming slow, short strokes all

while dipping one, then two, then three

fingers in her ass. When he did not get

any push back, he pulled out and ran his

thick head against her rim.

Andrea looked back with nothing

but unadulterated lust for her husband.

Greg was taking her to heights unknown

and she loved it. Usually she did not play

the rough sex game but tonight she was

playing for keeps. Her livelihood was on

the line and so was her marriage. He

pulled she pushed, he pulled she pushed,

just then she reached down to finger her

clit. Greg reached up and grabbed a

fistful of her hair and starting whispering sweet nothings in her ear. Andrea loved it and swore she had not had a better lover than Greg; as thoughts of another woman circled around in Greg's mind.

Greg dropped his load, turned Andrea around and told her to get dressed that he wanted to wine and dine on that ass at home. Greg stuffed his junk back in his pants and headed out the door and to the car.

They lived in a small community just 35 miles outside of Beaufort called Greenbow, which was actually on the border of Alabama. Far away from all the violence and drugs. Even though it was only occupied by the two of them, their house was modest. It was a brick structure that looked like it came from the pages of Better Homes and Gardens Magazine. There was a master suite with and attached master bath, three guest bedrooms with a full bath in each one, there were also two full baths down the hall, a living room, a study, a kitchen complete with a separate storage room for food, a large backyard with a swimming pool with an attached Jacuzzi. The garage could easily fit four cars. Greg had a small office built there with a separate entrance to the house. He used this as his man cave.

Upon arriving home, Andrea ran
to take a shower as she remembered that
they were supposed to go to Massey's for
their Thursday night festivities. After her
shower she came downstairs to find
Greg had not even started to get dressed.
He knew how she hated to be late for
Massey's she was she was scared she was
going to miss something. Andrea walked
behind her husband and put her arms
around his tight waist. She nuzzled her
nose into his back and inhaled his scent.
He always smelled so good and clean.
That amazed Andrea to no end that her
husband engages in filthy activities like
they did tonight and still smell crisp and

clean. For the first time in months, Andrea was considering skipping their Thursday night ritual and suggest they stay in and finish what they started at the store. Just when she was about to speak, Greg took her hands from his waist and headed upstairs.

Massey's was a small pub ran by Andrea's brother, Michael Harmony. His specialty was his homemade beer. He did it so well that he begged their father to front him the money to open the tavern. Greg and Andrea arrived at Massey's and, as usual, it was jumping. Everybody that was somebody was there. All the locals and politicians were there.

Every Thursday evening, the Mayor, local police, firefighters and even some of the wives would come out for drinks between seven and eight o'clock in the evening. After nine o'clock is when the real party began. The men would all send their wives home and the men would get some special treats. Michael would open the stage for some of the girls who needed extra cash, and they would dance or sing for the crowd. His only requirement was that the girls be scantily clad and sexy. His cut was 20 percent of what the girls took in, this was separate from their Thursday night tips, in which there was no overhead. Since the crowd consisted mostly of politicians and crooked cops, Thursday was payday for plenty of sexy ladies.

Andrea hated the fact that she was not able to participate in the festivities, and since she could not, she made it a point to pout, thinking that would stop Greg from sending her home with the Mayor's wife. She knew the program, Mrs. Mayor did not make a fuss, so why should she. Andrea was especially keen, since tonight was Thursday and it was also the night that Koffi worked and made the most tips. Andrea scoped the room for Koffi just as she was leaving to make sure she stayed

was a safe enough distance from Greg.
Andrea made her way over to Greg and
ran her hand up and down his chest; she
leaned in close to his ear and whispered,
all the while making eye contact with
Koffi. She Whispered, "Greg, please
don't be too long. I want to finish what
we started when you get home and I
want you to be able to perform when
you get there."

Massey's was a joint that was
passed down from one generation to the
other and Andrea's brother was owner
of the fine establishment, he wanted to
make sure to do like his dad, granddad,
great-granddad and great great-

granddad before him had done, and that is to one day pass the fine establishment to his sons.

As much as Andrea loved her brother's success, she was in no mood to deal with the locals. She loved the food, the drinks and the atmosphere of Massey's but, when happy hour took over, Andrea wanted nothing to do with the place. All she could think about was Greg taking her home so she could finish what she started back at the office. The more drinks Greg had, the more horny Greg got. Andrea loved him that way and he knew it. Andrea couldn't help but to think that Greg was going to give

Koffi all that drunk dick. Andrea hardly knew Koffi but that one thing she did know was that she hated her and wanted her to stay as far away from Greg as possible. If Andrea had her way she was going to do just that.

"I will be waiting for you to return to me my sweet, hurry up so that we can have a little night cap of our own when you get home. Greg you know I love your drunk dick and you know the drunker the better so bring it on home to mama."

Greg gave an exasperated sigh before turning Andrea toward the door and urging her to leave. Mrs. Mayor was beyond annoyed with Andrea; she could not understand how a woman could be so clingy. The way she saw it, as long as he is providing for home no need to worry what he did outside the home, she chopped it up to a man being a man.

KOFFI

CHAPTER IV...

*H*e stared as she finally made her way toward that door, he began to think, I thought I would never get rid of her. *I knew she was up to something but I was not in the mood. I love my wife but not the way she wants me to. I have never cheated on her, but I feel like she is smothering me. I feel like I cannot take a step, make a move or even breathe without her right up on me, I signed up for the long haul but for the first time I am having second thoughts.* Greg sighed as he returned to the reality of this being

Thursday night, the night where anything goes.

As Greg was downing his drinks all he could think about was how he had gotten to this point in his life. He was starting to have strange feelings about his marriage. When they first got married, it was like a dream come true for Greg. She was everything he wanted in a woman. Sexy yet sweet, innocent yet confident, strong but had a weakness that only he could console. They were inseparable and all Greg wanted was for her to bear his name and a child. She was what God intended for him to have as a woman, a wife and maybe someday...the mother of his child(ren). However, as time went on, they grew further apart. Something had changed, Greg changed, He wanted more emotionally, much more.

Greg wanted passion, a friendship and more fun. He needed a woman who wanted more of a spiritual connection than a sexual connection. Inside the bedroom, Greg made sure his woman was beyond satisfied. Greg and Andrea never had an issue within their bedroom, but as time went on, the sex between him and Andrea became routine. Eventually, Greg got bored and no longer wanted his wife or any woman for that matter, except Koffi.

"Hey Greg, so what'll it be," the bartender asked.

"Just the usual, Ray."

"You want me to bring your drink over for you?" Ray responded.

"No thanks, I will not be joining them tonight, In fact, do not allude to the fact that I am even here. Ray, let me ask you a question, is Koffi working tonight," Ray looked surprised that he asked about her because his usual routine consisted of him hanging with the in-laws.

"Yea, she's working tonight, what you want with her?" Ray said, with a concern laced tone.

"Relax man, I have something for her and told her I would drop it off. Plus, you know I'm a married man, Ray."

"Oh I know man, she is a good kid and you are not the first married man that comes in asking for Koffi, if you know what I mean. Just watch yourself man, you know how your brother in law gets. If he is not tapping that ass, then no one will. I am sure she will be out shortly. I'll have her to bring your drink over to your table."

"Thanks man, I appreciate that."

Greg headed over to the table in the corner that was situated near the juke-box, the lights were dim and it was out of the way. He knew where his in-laws were and as long as he sat in the corner, they would never see him. By the time they noticed he was still there, his father in-law would be on his third shot of whiskey and Michael, would keep the drinks coming as long as they were spending the money, anything to keep them happy.

Greg never understood how a child could allow his parents to get so drunk that they needed to go home. This was the norm for the Harmony men. Get drunk with their wives then send them home so they could be with their mistresses. It was so much of a routine it became a family tradition. This however, would prove to be a first for Greg. This was all so new to him.

"Here's the drink you ordered," the soft voice said, as she placed Greg's drink on the table.

There she was, just as beautiful as Greg remembered her from this morning. Koffi's body was so captivating that it left Greg mesmerized. He did not know if it was her smooth chocolate complexion or was it her soft butter lips. Her eyes were hazel brown with long jet-black curly eyelashes that, when she blinked, Greg's dick got rock hard. This girl had him in so many ways and she was not even aware of it.

"Greg is everything okay," Koffi asked.

"Yes Koffi, please sit down."

"I really shouldn't, you know how your brother in-law gets. He doesn't like us fraternizing with the locals."

"Let me handle him, I just need five minutes, Please?" Greg pleaded.

"Okay, just five minutes."

"Thank you, you know Koffi, I'm really sorry about Andrea this morning."

"Greg did you ask me to sit down to talk about your wife, If you did your time is up."

"No, I didn't, I want to get to know you, Koffi. I think, well I hope that...I guess what I'm saying is...."

Koffi looked at Greg with those big hazel eyes and that dazzling smile. She knew what Greg was trying to say. "Greg I don't think we should, I mean, I appreciate everything you do for me, but we shouldn't."

"Koffi, are you saying you feel nothing for me?"

"I do Greg, I really do, listen I have to go before he comes out here and makes a scene. I need this job."

"Why did you give me your address?"

"I gave it to you to keep in touch. That's all," Koffi started to get up from the table.

Greg needed to do something to let her know he was serious. Greg quickly pulled Koffi by the arm, pulled her down on his lap, and started caressing her face with his index finger. While he was caressing her face he gently ran his thumb across her bottom lip. He leaned in for a small peck as an indication that he was really serious about pursuing her, the kiss they shared was so aggressive that her nipples became so erect when they pressed against Greg's chest. Her kiss set off a myriad of sparks and feelings, that was his confirmation that she was as into him as he was into her. Greg's hand slowly glided up Koffi's soft legs and reached the top of her panty-line, and then slowly back down to the hot spot between her thighs. Her soft moans told Greg that she was enjoying every minute of his touch. Her eyes let Greg know she wanted more.

"Greg no, we can't not here. Not right now," she softly moaned. Koffi pulled herself back in a panic and ran off.

As she ran off, Greg saw that Koffi had bumped into Michael coming out from the back room. He headed right in Greg's direction after seeing the startled look on Koffi's face.

"What's up brother, Is everything okay with you?"

"Yea everything is okay, you know me, just trying to help where I can."

"I see that, but what was Koffi doing at your table?" Michael asked.

He never missed a beat in his tavern. He monitored all the girls, especially Koffi. Greg never understood his brother- in-law's fascination with her, but it definitely was quite clear that Michael wanted Koffi for himself.

"I'm good brother; actually I should be getting home to your sister, see you tomorrow in church." As Greg got up from the table, he could tell all eyes were on him, as he was leaving his place in the corner of the bar.

While Greg headed for the door, he could not help but notice that Michael had Koffi pinned to the corner of the bar. All kinds of thoughts entered into his head trying to make sense of it. The one emotion he could not seem to shake was anger.

Inside the back office of Massey's

"So what was that all about with my brother-in-law?" Michael asked of Koffi.

"Michael I don't know what you mean."

"You know damn well what I mean. I saw the two of you cuddled up in the corner Koffi, how many times do I have to tell you to stay away from the men that come up in here, they're no good for you."

"Are you jealous because someone other than you is interested in me," Koffi snapped back.

Michael walked over to Koffi and backed her into the corner where the supplies were. He reached for her neck and began to choke her. "If I wanted you Koffi, without hesitation, you would be mine, do I make myself clear," he said through clenched teeth.

Koffi cracked a half ass smile and just glared at Michael as if to let him know that his grip was nothing. "You just don't want any man have me but yourself, what's the matter, Michael, you scared of a little competition?"

"Competition, baby Greg is not competition. As a matter of fact, let me show you who you have to contend with." Michael stepped back from Koffi and stalked over to his desk, he pulled out his gun who he respectfully nicknamed, "daddy" and cocked it back. He looked inside the chamber to make sure it was loaded and he made sure Koffi saw his every movement. Michael then stepped to Koffi and demanded she strip.

To Michael's surprise, she did just as he asked of her, but surprised him by the way of her sexual motions. Koffi began to do what she knew best...strip.

She danced for her boss as if she was on stage yet there was no music playing. Inside Koffi's mind, there was music. Every moment was her stage, her game and with her seductive dancing, she let Michael know exactly why her name was Koffi.

"Is this what you want, daddy?" Koffi asked, as she looked right into the chamber of Michael's gun, with a twisted smirk on her face. Michael was in a state of shock. He just knew she would cry and call out for help, but Koffi was a different kind of woman.

"Oh so you like to feel threatened Koffi, is that it?" Michael asked.

"Oh that doesn't threaten me, but I'm sure you feel real threatened right now because you don't scare me Michael, so here I am, come and get it. This is what you want, right? You want to fuck me so bad that you can taste it. I see how you look at me when I come to work. I also know the real reason you don't want me on that stage is because you want me for yourself. Well here I am baby boy, come taste me."

Michael did not know how to respond to how Koffi was acting. He never had any woman stand up to him after he brought 'daddy' out to get his point across. He did not know what to do. Koffi was right, he wanted her all to himself, but did not want to mistreat her. In fact, she gained his respect. She now had Michael at a disadvantage…she was making him weak. Michael took his gun and pointed toward the door for her to leave.

"Are you letting me go, Michael?"

"Just go ahead Koffi, before I change my mind," he said sounding defeated.

"Why the sudden change of heart Michael, You don't want me?"

"Koffi, I'm going to say this one last time, leave my office and go home for the night. Do not worry about tonight's tips. I will pay you for the night. Oh and Koffi, I do want you, but I respect your game more, now go!"

Koffi did not need to hear him twice. Koffi zipped up her uniform and headed for the door. She looked back at Michael and cracked a smile. The level of respect between the two of them was apparent within that moment. However, the relationship between Koffi and Michael from this point on would never be the same.

KOFFI

CHAPTER V...

On the way home, Koffi thought to herself just how close she came to death tonight. She had heard the stories of how Michael was with other women that he obsessed over. Koffi realized that Michael would not have hurt her. A hustler always respects another hustler's game. There are rules to this shit and respect is one of them.

I can't believe he didn't take me up on my offer. There hasn't been any man that could deny my advances, Koffi thought, as she started to walk home. It took her about forty-five minutes to arrive at her room from the tavern. Koffi prayed all the way that Mrs. Blackstone was asleep by the time she got there. All she wanted to do was get Lance and go to her room.

As Koffi approached her home, she noticed a black town car trailing behind her, which was not out of the norm for this neighborhood. As she got closer to the brownstone, the closer the car got. Koffi was no stranger to violence so she surprised the driver by turning around and letting the person know she knew they were there. Koffi walked over to the car as it came to a complete stop.

"Greg, are you following me," Koffi asked.

Greg rolled down the window and motioned Kofi to get in the car. "Koffi, I'm sorry; I just had to see you."

"What do you mean you had to see me, you saw me out here walking in the freezing cold and you followed me instead of offering me a ride. Look Greg, you should not be here, but since you are, say what you have to say."

"Koffi it's cold, can you please just get in the car so we can talk? You can leave after I have my say, please. At least show me the courtesy of saying what I have been wanting to say for so long now, after I speak, I will leave the ball in your court as to what happens next."

Koffi looked at Greg, she walked around to the passenger side of the car and got in. As soon as she got in she started rubbing her hands together and putting them in front of the heat so they could get warm.

"What happened back at Massey's, I came to apologize. I misbehaved and I should not have let it happen. I am truly sorry."

"Well I appreciate that. I do, Greg. You came all the way out here to tell me that. I mean, c'mon, you can talk to me. I am a real good listener."

"Koffi, I appreciate that, but I must get home to my wife before she sends the troops out looking for me."

"You don't sound too convincing, Greg. So, you expect me to think that you came all this way to apologize about what we shared back at Massey's to just go home to your wife? No you did not Greg, Tell Koffi what you came here for?"

The tone in Koffi's voice had Greg at attention. Greg's thoughts started flooding him and his mind was all over the place. Greg looked at Koffi with care and concern, laced with lust. He felt a stir in his loins. He tried to ignore it but all attempts proved to be futile. By the tone in Greg's voice, he needed Koffi tonight and she was not about to let him down.

"Koffi, I was hoping that we could be more than just friends. I mean, you have been coming into the soup kitchen now for months and I feel like we have a connection. Don't you feel it, too?"

"I do Greg, just I came here for a reason and until I get what I want, I really want to stay low key."

"May I ask what it is that you came to Socoma Springs for, are you from here?"

"I guess you can say that I am, I came back to find my birth mother, I know she's still here in town."

"Koffi, I can help you with that if you let me. I know many people here in town, Andrea doesn't have to know."

"Oh Greg, I appreciate that, but this I must do alone. There is so much that I know and do not know that I think it would be best if I did it alone. Can you understand," Koffi said, as she grabbed Greg's hand.

"Koffi, you don't have to do this alone, please let me help you. I promise I will behave," Greg said, as he laughed aloud like a boy with his first real crush. I won't expect anything from you, I promise, just friendship. So can I help you?"

"So, we are just going to be friends, right?" Koffi responded.

"If that's what you want, then that's what it will be. It will be hard, but I can handle that." Greg smiled.

"I really appreciate it Greg, I really need to make this happen for me. Any help you provide my son or myself would be much appreciated, Thank you"

Koffi said as she looked out into the night.

"You don't have to thank me, it's my pleasure."

That very moment something came over Koffi, and she leaned over to give Greg a kiss to say thank you for his gesture to help. As she was going in for a kiss on Greg's cheek, he turned and her lips brushed his. It was at that moment that something in Koffi had been ignited.

"Koffi you said you didn't want this." Greg's moans were so strong that he sounded like a dog in heat.

"Greg, just sit back...let this happen..." Greg's manhood was already bulging through his pants. Koffi had motioned for Greg to let the seat of his car back as far as it would go. She mounted him while his hands were all over her body. One would have thought he had an extra pair of hands. She leaned down and began to kiss his lips and she moved downward toward his neck. "Is this what you want, baby?" Koffi whispered softly in his ear as she unzipped Greg's pants exposing his erect manhood. "Damn, baby, is all this love for Koffi?" she smiled with anticipation.

Greg replied, "Yes it's all for you. What you gonna do with it?"

Koffi leaned back on the steering wheel, careful not to make a sound on the quiet street. Koffi loved the fact that she was limber and could move like a gymnast, this is one time having that skill would prove beneficial. Koffi quickly and smoothly went in for the kill; she adjusted herself so that she was in the sixty-nine position. Greg looked up in utter amazement when he realized he was face to face with Koffi's nectar. It was as if Greg had died and gone to heaven. He saw her snatch shaven clean and the lips poked out of the seams as if there was no room for both of them in the crotch.

Greg took the liberty of freeing the most beautiful set of lips he had ever seen, and he had seen plenty, but nothing compared to the sight before him right now. Greg snatched the thin fabric from those lips. Greg found himself licking his lips, just before going in for the kill. Greg was in over his head and he finally realized that Koffi had taken all of him in her hot waiting mouth. She slid her tongue up and down his shaft sending chills up and down Greg's spine.

"Damn, Koffi, I knew you were something special! My God, baby!"

Koffi's wet mouth took over Greg's manhood as if she was having one of her favorite treats for the first time. Koffi just made a humming sound, that sent vibrations on his dick and that surely drove him up a wall.

Greg drove his face so far into Koffi's sweet nectar, you would have thought he was trying to become one with her. Greg was going crazy trying to satisfy Koffi and trying to enjoy the head she was laying on him.

Up and down Koffi's mouth made love to Greg's dick. Greg grabbed

Koffi's long, jet-black hair and began to assist her with her motions.

"Don't stop, baby, don't stop."

Koffi was enjoying what was happening between her and Greg, she suddenly stopped and slowly turned around. She was now face to face with Greg and he was taking in the sight before him. She pushed him down, while she hiked up her skirt over her round plump ass. She slid down on Greg's manhood and she thought he was going to lose his mind.

Koffi was tight and although she had not been with many men, she knew what turned them on and what it took to please them. Koffi was riding Greg, like he was the prized pony at the County Fair, each time she came down, she would clench her lips and that drove Greg mad. Koffi looked up and saw that Greg was not looking at her; he had his eyes closed focusing on not busting a nut. She paused long enough to get his attention and she warned him not to close his eyes she wanted him tO see everything.

Koffi stopped and told Greg to sit back and watch. As she went in the back seat and cocked her legs open, she told Greg to relax and watch her. He could not believe what was happening, but he was enjoying the show.

Koffi slid long slender fingers inside her hot wet juices, she started to massage herself softly, and her eyes never left Greg's. Then, she took another finger and slid it inside, in and out, Koffi began fingering herself making Greg watch her perform. She then reached over, took her finger, and made Greg lick her juices off her finger. He gladly obliged.

Pulling him in the back seat of the town car, Koffi spread her legs widely so that Greg could have all access to her. Greg blown away by her actions, was digging in her so deep that he thought he would get lost. He was moving a little out of sync, but after about four strokes, they had found a rhythm.

"Damn, Koffi, you feel so good. I don't ever want you to stop," Greg said.

Koffi was matching Greg thrust for thrust as he grinded his in side of her tight and sweet walls.

"Yes baby, give Koffi all of her dick, you like how this pussy feels?" Koffi moaned, as she could feel Greg about to release.

Greg grabbed Koffi by her waist and reached around and pinched her nipples sucked on her hard nipples, which turned Koffi on and she transformed into another person. Koffi reached up and gently pushed Greg in an effort to tell him she wanted to change positions, she was face down ass up and Greg was like a kid in the candy store.

"Don't stop! Don't you fucking stop! You hear me, daddy?" Koffi let out moans that Greg never would hear from his wife's lips.

His thrusts from his dick matched Koffi's every grind. They kissed so passionately that it sent chills down Koffi's spine causing her tight wet walls to release the juices from their passionate encounter. They both wanted and needed this.

"Oh God, Greg! I'm about to..." Koffi screamed with excitement as her nails dug into Greg's seats. Her back arched and she matched his strokes as wave after wave of her orgasm took over her body.

"Yes Greg! Yes baby, don't stop me, just take it! Mmm, this dick feels so good, baby! Here it comes...here it...oh Greg, hold me....damn, baby! Oh sshhhiiittt!" Koffi let out a yell and Greg had to cover her mouth so that no one could hear them, although they were in the car.

"Let it go baby, I got you! Oh shit, Koffi, you're gonna make me cum..." Shit, Koffi! Mmm, baby...here it comes, Koffi! Sshhit!" Greg let out a loud moan as his body collapsed on top of Koffi's. Koffi was not finished with Greg just yet...

Koffi had started shuffling around in the car trying to gather her things. Greg pulled Koffi near him and he began to caress her and run his hands up and down her arm. He leaned in to kiss her and spoke as he reluctantly pulled away.

"Koffi, we can't let anyone know about this."

"Don't worry Greg, I promise you this secret is just between me and you, Okay?"

Greg nodded as Koffi made sure she had everything before she got out the car, she kissed Greg goodbye and then headed toward her room. Greg watched Koffi to make sure she got inside safely. Once she was inside, Greg drove off.

All the lights were off inside so she was almost safe of not waking up Mrs. Blackstone. Upon her arrival, Ms. Blackstone caught Koffi and told her that Lance was in the room with Trinity, because she had an important errand to run. Koffi had to make it to Trinity's room to get Lance and then back to her room. Mrs. Blackstone knew this was Koffi's late night at the bar so she did not mind her breaking curfew. Koffi crept up the stairs and made it to Trinity's room. Two silent taps was all it took before Trinity had gotten up and open the door.

"You're late, Koffi! You were supposed to be here an hour ago. What happened?" Trinity asked, as she let Koffi inside to get Lance.

"I know Trini, I know. I didn't mean to, but something came up."

"You mean something or somebody Koffi? I know how you get

down, girl," Trinity snapped back. "You can't have this child off schedule so just let him sleep and I will have him ready for you in the morning."

"Are you sure, Trinity?"

"Yes I am sure, go get a shower because we both know that it was somebody that kept you late. Next time, you will have to pay me. Now go before you know who wakes up and catches both of us."

"She already knows about our arrangement, she was the one that told me you had Lance, I don't know how she knows, but she knows. "Trinity, you are the best girl," Koffi whispered.

"Yea, yea...make sure when it's my turn, you hold my daughter down for me if I need you."

Koffi gave Trinity a hug, peeked outside of the door, and looked down the stairwell. It was so quiet you could hear a pin drop. Koffi slowly walked down the hall to her room and opened the door. Her key made a small annoying sound and she looked over her shoulder to make sure no one heard it.

Once it was clear no one heard her, she opened her door and went inside. Koffi took off her things, grabbed a towel and her lavender soap and started to wash off the scent of her and

Greg. She never meant to take it that far, but something inside of her wanted to go that far. As she finished washing, Koffi put her uniform on her chair for tomorrow and then slipped into bed. She could not help but have mixed feelings about what just took place. How would she feel when she saw Greg again? So many confused emotions were going on inside of her mind that she did not know how to deal with them. One thing she was torn about and would haunt her forever; could she have possibly just fucked her own brother?

KOFFI

CHAPTER IV...

$\mathcal{K}$offi sat up from her old iron bed, and planted her manicured cocoa brown feet on the cold hardwood floors while she listened to the constant drip from her broken sink that just wouldn't stop. As she stared towards the half painted shut window, the sun was creeping up and about to make its presence that morning. She raised her head with her eyes slightly closed, arched her neck and back just enough to allow the sun to comfort her face with its warm rays. Koffi then turned her body around as she glanced down at her bed cracking half of a smile. She looked up towards the ceiling as if she was speaking directly with God and whispered the words, 'Thank You.' She was happy that she finally found someone to fulfill her needs, but was conflicted with unanswered questions that lurked around in her daily thoughts.

She was glad that she earned enough tips last night to finally pay for her room, and the little help from her gentleman friend didn't hurt. He also provided her son with a brand new coat and one for her as well. So how does she repay him? Pleasing a man was Koffi's specialty. She knew what to do, and when to do it without him having to guide her. She was a pro at making a man feel good.

Overwhelmed with gratitude of the genuine care that was shown towards her and her son, Koffi slowly leaned in and began caressing his head with soft strokes, while her fingers touched upon every wave in his hair. Not wanting him to wake just yet, she slowly slipped off her light-blue camisole exposing her erect nipples as well the matching light blue thongs. Koffi and her smooth chocolate colored, perfectly shaped coca cola body started to give into her temptation as she quietly nestled under the man's shoulder that made her feel so special the night before. She felt safe, guarded and loved. Their bodies fit like a glove even though the iron bed was manufactured to only fit one person. She didn't mind because she was where she wanted to be and the warmth of his body took Koffi's mind off of all of her struggles and daily stresses of the world, even if it was a lie.

Koffi decided to take it further and show her gratitude by waking her knight up from a peaceful sleep with soft tender kisses down his chest as she took her right hand and began to stroke his thick manhood to full erection. She desired nothing more than to please this man for everything he has done for her and her son, even if he was Andrea's husband Greg.

Their passionate act the night before, led them back to Koffi's room as Greg came back for round two, which had Koffi sneaking him into her room while everyone was fast asleep. Greg wasn't supposed to be there and she was taking a big risk, but neither of them cared about the consequences, they just wanted to be together.

Using her body to get what she wanted out of a man was what she knew best. Ever since she came to town, Greg made sure he was nothing but extra nice to her. From helping her with her groceries at his store by taking care of the bill, to driving by on whim, to leave a treat or something special in the back of the building for her son, like the time it was so cold outside he drove her around just to help her with all of her errands son she would not have to take the bus. Silently he wished he belonged to her, but knew that could never be, mainly because his world was so different from hers. It would never work between them and they both knew it. Koffi's main purpose for coming back to Soccoma Springs was to find her birth mother and claim what was rightfully hers. She quickly found that Greg was very eager to help her with this quest and wouldn't allow anyone else to help her. But this made Koffi feel somewhat obligated to Greg, even though the one man, Michael in whom she truly desired was too dangerous for her. She knew it and Greg knew it too, which is why he never let Koffi out of his sight. This left her with so many conflicting and unanswered questions, but it never stopped her from inviting Greg to have his way with her as the sun was rising.

"Morning Baby," said Greg who really wasn't sleep, but instantly became aroused and had enjoyed every bit of Koffi's sweet tender kisses on his already erect manhood. He was fully awake and anxious to serve Koffi's needs.

"Slow down baby, Koffi won't run from you." She said as she turned over and arched her back giving Greg easy access to her warm nectar. Greg glided his wet tongue down the side of her body towards her brown sugar legs and across her thigh to taste what was sweetly tucked between her crossed legs.

Koffi's body started to tremble as she opened her legs and cried out soft moans while Greg planted soft wet kisses around her wet walls. Koffi tried to quietly grip the sides of her sheets. Greg took his time pleasing every inch of Koffi's body, and he didn't worry if someone would enter the room. In his mind he was in pure heaven just where he was and nothing else mattered. Koffi happily succumbed to his every kiss, his every lick and his every touch. They made love for what seemed like hours until their bodies collapsed in their own sweat, and they quickly fell fast asleep. As it got later and later in the day, Koffi and Greg were startled by loud banging at her door. It was Mrs. Blackstone.

"Koffi I know you're in there, Where is my damn money for your room?" Koffi jumped up in a panic shaking Greg to wake up.

"Koffi what's wrong baby?" Greg was still half asleep.

"Shhh, I think that old lady is at my door." Koffi quickly raised up to go answer her room door.

"Okay so go open the door. Oh I see, I'm not supposed to be up here. I mean you're a grown woman Koffi, we both are." Greg reached down for his boxers and pants that were lying on the floor next to the bed.

"Let me handle her okay? You have no idea how mean she can be towards me so please just go stand over there behind the door, and don't make a sound, please for me Greg?"

Koffi grabbed her shear see through red robe and headed towards the door, but not without making sure that Greg was decent and out of sight first. If Mrs. Blackstone caught him in her room she would make sure that Koffi would be out in the street, no questions asked. Koffi opened the door real slowly and stuck just her head out the door. She didn't want to give Mrs. Blackstone any reason to want to check her room.

"What do you want this time of morning? You don't have to bang on people's door shouting their business

out all up and down in these hallways."
Koffi said as she tied her robe tighter to
cover up her naked body.

"I came to make sure you didn't
have a man up here, that's right I saw
you, you ain't slick. I bet his wife would
love to hear all about what you and Mr.
Giselle were doing last night. What you
got behind this door Koffi? You better
not have anyone in this room." Mrs.
Blackstone said as she barged her way
into Koffi's room.

"Why are you so damn nosey?"
Koffi' took a scan of the room
wondering where Greg was hiding, he
was nowhere in sight.

Mrs. Blackstone had an evil grin on her face as if she held the winning hand at poker game. She forced her way into Koffi's room just to make sure there was no one else in the room with her, but mostly to be nosey.

"Look old woman. I wasn't out in anybody's car last night so mind your own business! Quit harassing me, now get out of my room." Koffi opened the door and had her hand at the tip of it holding it open to show Mrs. Blackstone the way out. She didn't care if it was her building or not, Koffi hated disrespectful people, especially if it was from another woman.

"You better not Koffi or your ass is out of here. You and that little boy of yours will be on the street," Mrs. Blackstone stated with a threatening tone.

"Yea, yea, get out." Koffi said as she slammed the door behind Mrs. Blackstone. At some point Koffi knew deep down inside that she didn't have all the money for her weekly payment this time around, and she desperately needed a place to stay. The tips were coming in but were still a little scarce and not as much as they used to be. The help from Greg, even though it was temporary helped her out a lot. Koffi also knew that this would not continue.

"Damn that is one nosey old woman." Greg said from behind Koffi's tiny closet door. "I almost suffocated behind that tiny door. We gotta get you a better place to live baby." He said with a smile on his face as he reached behind the tiny closet door and grabbed the white washcloth that was hanging on a small silver rack that was bolted behind the door. He washed his beard and face so he could finish getting dressed. Koffi walked back over to her bed, plopped down and started to ponder where the money was going to come from.

She watched Greg get dressed thinking to herself that he was such a sexy man, but not her cup of tea. Greg was too needy, a trait that Koffi found very unattractive. "You find something funny Greg? I can't be on the street with my son."

Greg finished washing up and walked over to Koffi, kneeled down between her legs, lifted her head up and softly kissed her full pretty lips. "You and your son will not be on the street, I meant what I said last night Koffi. I can help you if you want me too. But only if you want me too, and I will do whatever it takes to get you what you need." Greg said as he stood up and walked around to the other side of the bed, grabbing his shoes and leaving Koffi to her thoughts.

"Greg I can't let you help me, what about your wife? She hates me as it is and I don't make it a habit of sleeping with married me" Koffi said as her voice got low.

"It's just this isn't right, but it feels so right. I'm not even making any sense, but something about you makes me feel safe."

Greg stood up and kissed on her forehead and repeated to her, "only if you want me too Koffi, only if you want me too. Let me deal with my wife,

Friends remember?" Greg walked towards Koffi's room door, with his shoes in his hand, and peeked out to make sure the coast was clear. He looked back behind him to see the look on Koffi's face. She just smiled at him to let him know she was okay and he smiled back as he tip toed out of her room quietly shutting the door but managed to whisper back, "I got you and don't worry I will go out the back door."

Koffi nodded her head in agreement as she watched the door close. Greg shut the door and started to head down the stairs to go out the back door. He kept his shoes off so he wouldn't make any noise so Mrs. Blackstone couldn't hear him. Greg managed to get to the last step. He looked back upstairs wiping the sweat from his brow thankful he made it down the stairs without anyone noticing. He was a little less than ten steps away from the back door the he and Koffi had snuck the night before when he bumped into Mrs. Blackstone coming in from outside. Taking a pull from her black and mild, she stopped in her tracks and locked the backdoor. Greg wasn't going anywhere.

"Well look at what we have here, Mr. Giselle right? What are you doing in my building?"

"You know who I am Ronica." Greg said flatly.

Mrs. Blackstone walked up to Greg and exhaled smoke from her cigarette right in his face. "Oh I know who you are sugar. I know exactly who you belong too as well. Now I asked you a question, what are you doing lurking around in my building? You live on the other side of town. Why are you down here with us poor folks?" Mrs. Blackstone was all of five feet seven inches tall but had an attitude like a pit bull. It was said that she had a fetish for tall dark and handsome married men and loved to bribe them with sex or money, and Greg fit her appetite just right.

"Look, how much you want? I know its money you want," Greg started to step back from Mrs. Blackstone as she came closer towards him. Each time he stepped back, she came closer. Greg reached into his pants pocket and pulled out a roll of money nicely rubber banded together.

"Hmmm as tempting as that looks, baby put your money away it's no good here. Plus you don't have enough to keep my mouth shut. But then again, I can think of something else you can share with me, you know, spread the love around." Mrs. Blackstone had Greg pinned against the backside of staircase with no place to run. She was so close to him that their lips almost touched, that's when she started to grind on him causing his manhood to naturally rise.

"I know you were up there with that jezebel Koffi. You know she's tainted. You need a real woman not no little girl. You remember how we used to get down back in the day."

"Oh and who might that woman be Ronica," Greg turned his face away from hers.

"I know you still like me Greg, I can feel it. See we even on a first name basis. Let's take this back to my room and talk about some thangs, or I can show you right here, right now. You know we go way back, and you know I treated you remember?" Mrs. Blackstone started to laugh and lick her lips as she backed away from Greg looking him up and down like a piece of meat, giving him some air to respond.

"Ronica you know I will never sleep with you again. What we had back in the day was just that, back in the day. So don't flatter yourself." Greg said while putting on his shoe and motioning for the front door. When he opened the front door, he turned and looked back at Mrs. Blackstone laughing and said, "Never again," Greg glanced up at the top of the stairs to ensure that no one else, especially Koffi saw his little altercation with Ronica and walked out the door to his car that was parked in the back of the building.

Mrs. Blackstone just smiled to herself and walked back to her room and placed a call to someone who would be very interested in Greg's whereabouts...

KOFFI

CHAPTER VII...

Back in her room, flustered with so many thoughts, Koffi was already running late for her appointment down at the welfare office. She grabbed the white porcelain bowl that Greg just used, rinsed it out and refilled it with lukewarm water and started to wash up. Every time she touched herself, she thought about Greg and what had transpired that morning and the night before. She may have been in a rush to leave, but Koffi took her time. She always took pride in how she looked, smelled and dressed each and every day.

It took her about twenty minutes to clean herself, put on her black corduroys, with a black fitted camisole underneath. She covered it with a long white turtleneck sweater and slipped into her black shoe boots that she got from downtown at a local flea market last month. She walked over to her half sized mirror to give herself a once over. She put her long jet black hair into a ponytail before she left. She reached into her black leather bag that was hanging on the door knob of her room, and pulled out the sample bottle of Egyptian Musk oil that she five fingered a few weeks ago from one of the vendors while shopping with Trinity. She rubbed a few drops on her neck and her wrists. She glanced around her room to make sure she had everything, grabbed her black leather coat, opened her door and locked it heading towards Trinity's room to let her know she was leaving for the day. Trinity's room was only two doors down and she was already standing in from of her door with her arms folded, waiting for Koffi.

"You know I saw him leave your room right, Koffi are you crazy pulling some shit like that? Girl, get your ass in here and I want all the damn details." Trinity grabbed Koffi by the arm and pulled her in the room and made her sit on the bed as she helped little Lance get his things together.

"Girl I just needed to clear my head, you know."

"Cut the shit Koffi, I mean crap!" Trinity said as she lit her cigarette and blew out some smoke,

"I want all the fucking details Koffi!"

"I aint telling you nothing, cause your mouth is too damn big Trinity.

"You better watch yourself Koffi. You're playing with fire messing around with Andrea's husband. You know what she is capable of."

"Trini I will be just fine, don't worry okay? I will see you at work later tonight."

"Yea okay Koffi," Trinity said as she shut her door.

Koffi started to walk down the stairs to get Lance so she could take him to the bus stop for school. Koffi stopped when she saw the door to Mrs. Blackstone's apartment slightly cracked open; and she heard her talking loudly on the phone to someone. Koffi motioned for Lance to come to the front door so they could leave, but not without being blown away by what she heard in the conversation coming from Mrs.

Blackstone's place. As Mrs. Blackstone finished up her conversation, she noticed Koffi sneaking out with Lance.

"Next time knock on the door when you see grown folk talking." Mrs. Blackstone said as she slammed the door and went back in her room to make another phone call. Dragging her feet back over to her phone that sat by her living room window, she called Lois. "Hello, is this Lois Harmony?"

Koffi grabbed her son and rushed out the door. Koffi had Lance bundled up tight as Koffi noticed Lance's bus pulling up early. She ran with lightning speed with little Lance trying to keep up behind her to screaming for the bus to wait. "Wait, wait…"

"Ms. Simpson, you're not usually late, is everything okay?" Terry the bus driver asked as she opened the doors to the yellow school bus. "Hey shut up back there!!" she screamed at the kids making noise on the bus.

"Okay baby mommy loves you, be a good boy okay."

Lance gave his mommy a big hug and said, "I will mommy."

"Hi Miss Terry," Koffi said to the bus driver.

"Be on time next time Koffi."
Miss Terry responded and closed the
doors as she pulled off.

Koffi watched her son's bus ride
down the street as she bundled her coat
up tight as the wind chill shot straight
through her body. Koffi began her walk
to the bus stop, she had to catch the bus
in the opposite side of where Lance's but
picked him up. She briskly walked, and
as she walked past her building she
noticed Mrs. Blackstone staring out her
front window with a devilish smirk on
her face. Koffi thought to herself as she
shook her head, "This town is just too
damn small." Just then Koffi looked up

and noticed Andrea Harmony getting out of her car.

"What the hell is she doing here?" Koffi thought to herself.

KOFFI

CHAPTER VIII...

$\mathcal{G}$reg jumped in his car and headed for Harmony Hands to help open up. He started the car, pulled out of the back of the building, and began to make a right turn, when he noticed his wife and mother in law across the street with Koffi headed towards their direction. "What the hell are they doing here?" Greg thought to himself. Instead of taking the right, he made a u-turn and parked his car two blocks down the street from Mrs. Blackstone building. He wanted to see exactly what Koffi would do and more importantly what his wife and crazy ass mother-in-law would do. He knew Koffi could hold her own, but wasn't sure what she would do when it came to his mother-in-law.

Koffi pretended she didn't see either one of the women, especially Andrea. She found it very odd, and too much of coincidence that Andrea and whomever this woman was, showed up right after Greg left. "Did he send her here, did he tell her about the night and the morning we shared?" Koffi thought. Koffi headed towards the bus stop to head down to Social Services, which was about a block away from where she puts her son on the bus, but two blocks away from her room. It was sunny but breezy and Koffi didn't want to be bothered with any of this shit this morning. She had too much on her mind.

"Excuse me Miss," the mystery woman asked.

"Yes," Koffi responded as tried to keep walking past them so she could wait for the bus.

"Yea that's her Momma, that's the cunt that always comes in the store and Greg is always going out of his way to help her." Andrea said as she pointed to Koffi.

Andrea's mother walked right behind Koffi as she antagonized her all the way to the bus stop. Andrea was a lot of talk, but her mother was a different person. Andrea's mother was a sassy and vindictive woman. If she had to come to you about her daughter Andrea, she made sure you felt her wrath. Andrea and her mother were very different, yet Andrea was sassy like her mother, she just couldn't back it up like her mother.

"Yes I am talking to you; I understand that you and my daughter have a problem, Is there a problem?" Andrea's mother asked as she grabbed Koffi's arm to make her stop walking.

"Let go of my arm please, I don't want any problems, your daughter has a problem with me because her husband is nice to me and my son. That's her problem not mines. What's the matter Andrea, you had to run and get your mother to handle your affairs after I whooped your ass the first time? You must enjoy getting beat!"

"You aint whoop nothing sweetheart," Andrea yelled back as she tried to grab Koffi but her mother stopped her.

"Little girl you did what to my daughter?"

"Look lady, you seem like an intelligent woman and I know you didn't come all the way down here to ask me what the problem is with your daughter, what is it that you want, you obviously want something from me, so what is it because my bus is coming."

Andrea's mother walked up to Koffi looking her up and down. She pushed Andrea back so she couldn't hear what she whispered into Koffi's ear. "Leave my daughter's husband alone, I know your kind, See you remind me a lot of myself when I was your age. Do yourself a favor, stay far away from Greg Giselle or else."

The number twenty-eight bus started to get closer to where Koffi was standing. Andrea's mother the backed up from Koffi with a sneaky grin on her face as if what she told Koffi was to scare her.

Koffi walked away from Andrea's mother and as the bus stopped and opened the doors to let Koffi on. Koffi turned around with a smile, "Lady do yourself a favor and go teach your little girl over there how to keep her husband happy, the she wouldn't have to worry about women like me. Your threats mean nothing to me. I'm a grown woman and Greg is a grown ass man. If I wanted him I will have him and there is nothing you or your daughter will be able to do about it." Koffi stepped on the bus, opened up her backpack ad took out her dollar fifty to put in the money slot on the bus and turned around to wave goodbye to Andrea and her mother as the doors closed on the bus.

Andrea and her mother stepped back from the bus as they watched it drive past them blowing smoke in their faces.

"Momma, how could you just let her speak to me like that, and you just let her get on the bus? Exactly what did you say to her?" Andrea asked as she started to walk back to the car.

"She got my point. But she was right about one thing. You can't keep calling me every time Greg strays. I taught you better than that. Luckily Ronica was concerned enough to call me about her suspicions."

"Ronica called you for what?"

"Never mind that what kind of name is Koffi anyway," Andrea's mother asked as she walked to her baby blue Bentley and got in. She reached into her purse and pulled out her little silver flask and took a sip.

'Momma you can't drink and drive, do you have to do this first thing in them morning, oh and I can't go with you to meet daddy." Andrea said as she got on the passenger side and shut the door. "Momma you really shouldn't be drinking this early in the morning.

"I didn't ask you for your thoughts Andrea. Why can't you come to breakfast with us? And exactly how much do you know about this girl?"

"Because I have to meet someone, and I don't know much, just that she has no one but her son. She has no family here at all. It's rumored that she has a brother, but you know how this town is. The rumors are just that, rumors made up by these nosey ass people in this town." Andrea said while turning her face up in disdain.

"Yea I bet, you better hope Greg don't catch you. Hmmm, well I will just have to keep my eye on her. Do you even know her full name; maybe I can have one of my friends down at the town clerk's office look up some information on her for me." Andrea's mother said as she turned the key in the ignition.

"I heard her last name is Simpson, she has some weird middle name, not southern at all. Koffi Safiya Simpson is her name, that's it. Momma what's wrong? You look like you just saw a ghost."

Lois' voice caught in her throat with the mention of Koffi's name, as an air of recognition registered on her face. Lois sped out of her parking spot and rushed to her destination.

"Andrea what did you say her name was," Lois asked.

"I said Koffi Safiya Simpson, something weird like that, why?"

"No reason. I just want to make sure the name is right for when I go to the clerk's office." Andrea kept thinking in her mind, there's only one girl she knew with that middle name and it just couldn't be her. It just couldn't be. After witnessing the exchange between his wife, his mother in-law and Koffi, Greg headed for Harmony Hands.

KOFFI

CHAPTER IX...

*D*owntown at Fiske Breakfast Den, sat William Harmony, the richest man in town next to the Mayor. He was always dressed in a three-piece suit with the shoes to match. Stacey Adams was his favorite to wear. He had different gold cuff links to wear every day of the week; clean-shaven with a walk so smooth it made the women in this town crave attention from him. He was a light caramel complexion with jetblack wavy hair that he kept cut low. It was rumored he was mixed with Indian, but it was just a rumor. Even though William was married to sneaky ass Lois, he loved the attention from the ladies, but he never strayed. But there was one thing he loved more than women and more than his wife, his money. William had done very well for himself with several Bed & Breakfasts that he had opened with his wife Lois. Only problem was William made the money and his scandalous wife, Lois would screw the help and blow the money, a dangerous combination that was spiraling out of control. Every Monday morning, William would have breakfast with his wife, Lois and their daughter Andrea down at Fiske. It became somewhat of tradition. They served good food, and were well known for their pecan waffles. But William went to see the young women, even though he claimed they had the best tasting eggs he had ever tasted. Sometimes Lois made it and sometimes she didn't; it all depended on who she was doing that morning.

"Sir would you like to order now, or do you want to continue to wait for your wife and daughter," the waitress asked a growingly impatient William Harmony.

"No they can order on their own when they get here, I'll have the number two with my eggs scrambled hard please."

"Okay and would you like coffee or juice with your platter?"

"I'll take coffee, Black please."

"You got it big daddy," The waitress said as she winked at William and pinched his cheeks.

"Awww shucks girl you're gonna make me leave my wife, Stop playing around with Big William."

"Did I just hear you say you would leave me William?" Lois said as she walked in and sat down at her husband's table.

"Yea and I'm taking my money with me too," William said laughing out loud.

"Well dear you can try, but you won't live to see a dime the way you drink."

"Whatever baby, whatever happened to good morning baby or hey baby did you miss me?"

"Awww does Daddy William need some attention today?"

"Well it would be nice to get some from my wife, But she's too busy with the...."

"Don't you even say it William, we have had this discussion already, so hush! If you want attention go get it from your mother, I am not in the mood today."

"You're never in the mood for me. But you see this nice young lady here that is serving me this damn good cooked food, well she will show me some attention, won't you darling?" William said to the waitress as she set his platter of eggs, sausage, grits and jelly toast in front of him while giving his wife the rolling of the eyes.

"Sweetie if you want him you can have him," Lois said as she started to eat from William's plate.

"Lois you have such a nasty disposition, but I do love you, that I do, now order your own damn plate and get out of mine. And I thought you were coming with Andrea, where is she?

"Oh I dropped her at the store; she had something she needed to handle."

"Yea I bet, if she is anything like her momma, she being handled alright."

Back at Harmony Hands

"Listen, what you are going to do about her, she and Greg are spending way too much time together and I don't like it. Momma even had words with her this morning, wait a minute hold on...."

Andrea poked her head from out of the office because she heard a noise, but when she looked down the hall she didn't see anyone.

"Yea I'm back, I thought I heard something, No I'm okay. Listen, we need to talk face to face. Yea I can be there tonight. Okay...bye." Andrea hug up the phone and headed out to the front of the store to open the door. As she walked up front she noticed him standing at the door gazing through the window.

"I'm sorry, but we are not open yet, you have about fifteen more minutes. Come back then okay," Andrea yelled through the stained glass door pointing down the closed sign.

"Miss I need your help, I am looking for a young lady that comes here quite often. I was hoping to catch her this morning. Can you help me please," the man said as he was reaching for something in his pocket.

Andrea hated to interact with the strays that would come down to Harmony Hands, because she felt she was better than them. She would serve them, but she wanted no parts in dealing with them personally. But she knew deep down inside, if it were her husband, he would help. Since she didn't want to hear about it later, she decided to open the door.

"Oh dear lord hold on," Andrea went to go grab the store keys from the back to open the door to let the gentleman in.

"Thank you, you are far too kind, it's cold out there, he said blowing into his hands. I'm sorry my name is Stanley, Stanley Hinson, and you are pretty lady," he asked as he extended his hand to shake.

Andrea was completely mesmerized by this handsome well-groomed, tall chocolate colored skinned man standing before her. He stood about six foot three, with a deep dimple on the left side of his cheek. He had one diamond earring in his ear, a silver necklace with a diamond cross that sat outside of his suit. He reminded Andrea of her father, and how every woman in town thought he was sexy. But this man had Andrea's undivided attention he just didn't know it. She was under his spell. Andrea left his hand extended and walked back around behind the countertop towards the register.

"My name is Andrea, Andrea Giselle; this store belongs to me and my husband. You don't look like any stray from around here, and you sure aren't dressed like one. Now I know everybody, and I don't know you. I don't ever recall seeing you around here. What brings you to Beaufort?" Andrea asked as she started to put fruit in one of the baskets that sat on top of the counter.

"Well I live about fifty miles from here and I'm searching for a friend of mine, I was told she moved here. Maybe you know her. If I show you a picture of her, do you think you would you recognize her?" Stanley responded as he took the folded picture out of his wallet and put it out for Andrea to see.

Andrea snatched the picture from Stanley and glared at it for a few seconds. "Gimme that picture, I know everybody so yes I..." she stuttered moving backward slowly

"Something wrong pretty lady," Stanley asked as he lit a cigarette and exhaled smoke. "Do you know her, Oh I'm sorry do you mind me smoking in your establishment?"

"Yea I know of her and yes I do mind so please put it out. Why are you looking for her," Andrea asked as she threw the picture back at Stanley, handing him an ashtray from the shelf behind her.

"I'm sorry as you wish pretty lady, well judging by your attitude; I'd say that you probably can help me set up a meeting with her. The way you responded I'd say I came to the right town. Nobody gets under anyone's skin like she can, but she can't know I'm here. It's kind of a surprise, so uh can you help me pretty lady?" Stanley said as he turned on his charm.

"Yes I can help you, but what's in it for me," Andrea said with a sly smile

Stanley let out a devious laugh, walked around the partition to where Andrea was standing, and was now standing face with Andrea with no barrier. She didn't budge. It was almost as though Andrea wanted Stanley to touch her. Stanley glided his index finger slowly down the side of Andrea's left cheek, going all the way to her middle button of her blouse. Andrea's eyes never left Stanley's for one second.

"Oh I think we can come up with something," He said as he unbuttoned that middle button.

Andrea smiled as she moved closer to Stanley rubbing her hard nipples that were peeking through her sweater up against his chest, "I think we can Mr. Stanley....I think we can," she said with a squeal of delight.

Stanley leaned in and kissed Andrea as if she was his woman. Andrea happy to receive any attention threw all the brown paper bags, baskets of fresh fruit and business cards that were on the countertop to the floor and leaned back against the countertop as Mr. Stanley started to unbutton Andrea's blouse one button at a time. Kissing each other passionately with no regard to who could walk by the store and see all that was going on, they continued this lustful act on top of the countertop. Stanley took his hat and coat off, he undid his tie, and Andrea ripped open his shirt, sending his buttons flying around the store. Both of them were so turned on by their bodies touching one another. Stanley handled Andrea's body like she was a precious gem that could break if he dropped it. Stanley scooped Andrea up and sat her on top of the counter and continued to have his way with her. Laying her back until she was completely flat, and her blouse completely open exposing nothing but her light pink lace bra and erect nipples that were clearly ready to be sucked. She gave in to Stanley's demands and she allowed him to handle her hot body. Stanley kissed her from the top of her neck, then making his way down lifting up her bra up, and began to circle her nipples with his hot tongue causing Andrea's body to tremble all over. "Damn, what woman wouldn't enjoy this type of loving from her man," Andrea said as she let out a soft moan as he continued to kiss her making his way down to her belly button.

"Just enjoy it pretty lady...enjoy it." Stanley said as he made his way to the hem of her skirt and started to raise it up her thighs. Spreading her legs, she let Stanley finger her to the point she released all of her juices onto his fingers as her body glided back and forth on his fingers, as if she was fucking the real thing.

Andrea had never felt this way before and she had no idea who this man was and why he was doing this to her, but it felt good. Andrea was still young, all of twenty three years old, and even though he wanted her own husband, Greg to make her feel this way, it would never happen again. All she knew was that her body needed some attention and she didn't seem to care whom it came from, even if was from a strange child molester from another town.

Andrea and Stanley continued on with their consensual acts without a care in the world, not realizing that standing around the other side of the store in the storage room was Andrea's husband Greg, who was quietly counting the new shipment of canned goods that had just come in. Greg got the surprise of his life when he turned on the security screens; his wife was having sex with a strange man in the front of the store.

KOFFI

CHAPTER X...

Downtown at the local Social Services building the lines were going around the corner. Everyone here was either getting food stamps, rent paid or to see their child.

"Dammit, I should've come earlier," Koffi said as she got off the bus and headed to the back of the long line.

"Get used to it girl, this is how it is at the beginning of every month." The strange woman said.

"I've never had to do this before so I don't know how it is, but thanks."

Koffi responded as to end the conversation before it got started.

Koffi just stood there as she watched dozens of women with their children in tow waiting patiently to get inside. Some women with two and three children by their side; some of them had one on their hip, the other in the stomach and the last holding the hand. It was a sight to see. A sight that Koffi was not used to, but for some strange reason she felt comfortable. It was a small brick building with just two glass doors. They were calling people in four at a time. When it was finally Koffi's turn she was seen by a Caucasian woman that was about five feet three inches tall, heavy in weight, dirty blond hair and glasses. She escorted Koffi to the back and told her to have a seat and the pulled out a stack of paperwork and placed it in front of Koffi.

"My name is Ms. Peterson, and I will be your case worker, so what can I do for you?" she asked as she never looked in Koffi's direction.

"Well I came to see if I could get help with some food and assistance with my room and board."

"Where are you staying, and I will need the social for you and your dependents." Ms. Peterson started to take notes and entered it into the computer system.

Koffi with a look of confusion on her face because she didn't think she needed it and she didn't want anyone to know of her past; so she played dumb like she didn't know what Ms. Peterson was talking about. "You mean my...social...security...number?"

"Yes, as in your social, what is the number baby because I have to enter it into our database to track you."

"Ma'am I don't know what it is."

"Okay did you lose it or can you get it, and bring it in, I can't help you without it, and you will need it for any dependents you need assistance for as well." Ms. Peterson started to put the stack of papers to the side.

"Look I need help. I'm staying over at The Green Garden rooming house and ..."

"Chile, are you talking about Ronica's house?" Ms. Peterson said with a strange look on her face.

"Yes why? And why the hell are you looking at me like that?"

"Because if you're staying there then you don't need my help because, Ronica gets a check for each one of her tenants. It is part of the Government program that we started a few years back. That's how she is able to keep the old run down place. She's supposed to deduct the room and board and provide you with a small allowance for personal items. But it also includes food. So if I were you, I'd run up outta here because she can get in a lot of trouble sending you down here. Wait, she has to have your information baby in order to get a check. Let me see if I can find out, what was your first and last name again?"

"But she didn't send me here, and she knows nothing about this. I'd like to keep it that way if I could please. So can you help me or not?"

Ms. Peterson let out a long sigh and leaned back in her chair and started to size up Koffi. She started to rumble through her papers to search for a number.

"I know of a guy who might be able to help you. But you never got this name or number from me. His name is Stanley, Stanley Hinson. Look him up, and... Miss Simpson? Miss Simpson?"

Ms. Peterson got up from her chair and looked out into the long office hallway to see where Koffi went and her co-worker came out from his office and said, "You looking for that girl that was just in your office?"

"Yea, did she leave?"

"Like a bat out of hell," The co-worker said as he wheeled his chair back into his cubicle

Koffi ran like her life depended on it. She saw the name that Ms. Peterson was writing down on the paper and as soon as she saw the last name, a chill ran down her spine and the hairs stood up on her arms. How could she possibly know him? Koffi began to reconsider Greg's offer to help he find and build the estranged relationship with her biological mother. This was the only way that she could claim what was rightfully hers, even if it meant doing

battle with her own family.

KOFFI

CHAPTER XI...

Making her way back to her room, Koffi's mind started racing with the harsh reality that the one man she was trying to escape, was close by. Did he always know about her real mother? Koffi's distain for this man grew every day since he first betrayed her. The countless nights he entered her room and abused her body yet claiming to praise the Lord was a daily reminder of what he was capable of. But what could she do. She was a child. Helpless, with no one there to save her from this monster, she gave up her strength and let him have her, but all the while plotted her escape. This was her mission in life, find her mother and ask her why?

Koffi stopped the first bus stop she saw that would take her back to her room. Tonight she just didn't feel like working at Massey's or dealing with Michael's sexual advances. Spotting the one seat by a window, Koffi sat down and let out a long heavy sigh. All she could think about was being in Greg's arms. The warmth of his skin, his scent and his butter lips were all she could think about. He didn't love his wife and he proved that time and time again every time he was with Koffi.

"Next stop please."

Koffi made it back to her room safe and sound. Koffi had just enough time to take a nap before Lance was to come home from school. She didn't know what her next move was and to even think about Mr. Hinson being in town hurt her head all the more. As she crossed the street she already noticed Mrs. Blackstone peeking from her front window. That's the last person Koffi wanted to see, but knew she needed to pay her. Koffi entered the boarding house and sure enough, Mrs. Blackstone's door was wide open as she always left it except when she was sleeping. It was almost as if she was waiting just for Koffi to come home. All the other tenants were gone for the day, either at a state mandated program or at a job that she was able to get for them. So it was just her and Koffi, that is until Trinity came home from her job which would be in about an hour. Koffi heard Mrs. Blackstone talking loudly on the phone, so this was a perfect time to try and sprint to her room.

"I know right! But you know she messing around with James brother right? Helen, hold on, one of my tenants just walked in. No, girl, just hold on, we need to finish talking... okay." Mrs.

Blackstone put her phone down and headed towards her door. She watched Koffi creeping up the stairs to her room but was not about to let her get away without a warning. "You got my money girl?"

Koffi stopped in her tracks and let out a long sigh. She turned around with an exasperated look on her face, "Yea what about it?" Koffi was not in the mood for her shit today.

"You have been ducking me ever since this morning. What's the matter, you were sassy this morning when your little friend was here. You know his wife knows about you and where's that bastard child of yours?"

"Leave my baby out of this Ronica. Yea... I know you're first name and all the mess you are involved in. I promise you wont get away with it."

"You think you so damn smart do ya? You know everything right? Well, if you know so much, where's my damn money at? I'm running a boarding house not a whorehouse like your mama did... Oh did I touch a nerve?"

Ronica glared at Koffi with a sinister smile aand walked back into her apartment to continue her conversation on the phone with the door still wide open so Koffi could hear her talking. "Yea girl I'm back. I had to set one of my tenants straight…"

Koffi stood there with confusion on her face. *My mama?* Koffi ask Ronica what she meant but with her room not being paid she knew she wouldn't get any straight answers. All Koffi could do is make good on her plan to find out the truth and there was only one person she could turn to at this point. Koffi made her way upstairs to her room passing Trinity's room wishing she was there so she could talk to her about her next move. That would have to happen later. Right now Koffi decided to take a chance and reach out to the woman she always knew as her mother to gain more insight about her family tree. An hour had passed and little Lance was home from school. Just as excited as little Lance was ready to share his day to his mother, Koffi was just as excited to hear it, but her mind wouldn't allow her to get past what Ronica said earlier about her mother. After everyone was sound asleep, Koffi snuck out to go to the payphone in the back of the boarding house where Ronica had it hidden from everyone. Trinity had told Koffi about when she first got there and to only use it at night because that's when Ronica unlocks it. Why it was locked up during the day, Trinity never explained.

Koffi made her way outside as fear immediately set in. This was her only way out and closer to the truth.

Please be home. Please don't let him answer the phone... "Ms. Hinson... Mom, yea it's me Koffi. I need you're help..."

KOFFI

For New Release updates,

our blog, and more visit:

www.sheridanbrownpress.com

Social Media:

Facebook:

facebook.com/SheridanBrownPress

Twitter:

@SheridownBrownPr

Instagram:

@SheridanbrownPress

Email:

sheridanbrownpress@gmail.com

www.ingramcontent.com/pod-product-compliance
Lightning Source LLC
Chambersburg PA
CBHW061137170626
46809CB00003B/897